First published in Great Britain in 2009

British Library Cataloguing-in-Publication Data
A CIP record for this title is available from the British Library

ISBN 978 1 84114 958 5

HALSGROVE
Halsgrove House,
Ryelands Industrial Estate,
Bagley Road, Wellington, Somerset TA21 9PZ
Tel: 01823 653777   Fax: 01823 216796
email: sales@halsgrove.com

Part of the Halsgrove group of companies
Information on all Halsgrove titles is available at: www.halsgrove.com

Printed and bound by Grafiche Flaminia, Italy

Contents

For Amanda and Toby

Introduction

The Lake District as a national park has only existed since 1951; Cumbria as a county, since 1974. But the old titles of Cumberland and Westmorland were collectively known as Cumbria for centuries and the mountainous Lakeland heart was an integral part of the region's fabric. The national park status of the Lake District has defined the region for many visitors but Cumbria has always been a richly diverse and historic county with great rewards for those who go looking. Of course there has always been more to Cumbria than the "Lakes' but for many visitors the bigger picture is less well known.

Cumbria's landscapes are defined by its geography. It is literally surrounded by uniqueness – the vast wildlife sanctuary of Morecambe Bay defines the southerly border whilst the remote Pennines hem the east; Hadrian's Wall separates Cumbria and England itself from Scotland's wild borders to the north leaving the Irish Sea to wash the west coast.

Here, then is a journey through the landscape of Cumbria. A county of breathtaking beauty, grandeur and surprise that includes the Lake District but reveals also the less frequented landscapes of the Eden Valley, the Eastern dales and Lune Valley, the Borders to the Solway Firth and West Cumbria to Morecambe Bay. It offers an insight into the county that is home to "Britain's favourite travel destination" but this is not the Lake District - this is Cumbria.

The Eden Valley

Any place that calls itself Eden clearly has a lot to live up to and this fertile river valley manages to do justice to its title. Bounded by the harsh and remote Pennines to the east and the Lake District fells to the west, the Eden Valley follows the course of the River Eden with a mixture of verdant green farmland, traditional market towns and red sandstone villages, some dating back to the Vikings. In fact this region was settled long before that and there's plenty of evidence of prehistoric activity in the form of stone circles, henges and earthworks; Mayburgh Henge and King Arthur's Round Table at Eamont Bridge outside Penrith are prehistoric; as is Long Meg and her Daughters, near Little Salkeld, said to be the third largest stone circle in Britain.

The River Eden itself rises in the Mallerstang Valley at the southern end of the Eden Valley, flowing nearly 100 miles north to empty into the Solway Firth near Carlisle. It enjoys a reputation as one of the finest salmon and trout rivers in the North of England amongst those who know about these things but keeps its secret guarded and remains less frequented than other rivers. However, it is well known for riverside walking, away from the more challenging terrain of the fells and mountains of the Lakes. Lacy's caves, carved out of sandstone on the riverbank at Lazonby and the sandstone gargoyles and scrolls at Armathwaite are often visited and the Eden Benchmarks, ten intriguing sculptures, set in particularly well chosen settings form a sculpture trail and act as resting places from which to appreciate the river.

The Settle to Carlisle Railway, the most scenic in England, runs through the Eden Valley with stations at Appleby and Kirkby Stephen which make it a viable mode of transport from which to explore the river and market towns. Appleby in particular is worth the trip. Famous for its annual horse fair where gypsy travelers from every corner gather to do business as they have done since 1685, trading horses and anything else you can think of, Appleby is also exceptionally pretty, historically interesting with its castle and medieval buildings and important locally as it was once the county town of Westmorland.

If the Eden Valley were transplanted to any other county, it would in itself be much admired and sought out. But it forms a boundary to the Lake District National Park and inevitably it has been overshadowed. Perhaps that's a pity, perhaps not – it remains relatively unspoiled, peaceful and free from the traffic and chaos that routinely blight the honey-pots of the Lake District and is perhaps blessed after all.

Opposite
Bright yellow oil seed fields near Penrith provide a foreground for the Pennines beyond. At 893 metres (2,930 ft), Cross Fell is the highest point in the Pennine hills and also the highest point in England outside of the Lake District.

Bright winter sun picks out the ribbon of the Orton Fell road which traces a lonely path across Great Asby Scar to Crosby Garrett.

Winter frost etched onto the limestone pavement on Great Asby Scar, considered to be one of the best examples of karst scenery in Britain and a National Nature Reserve.

A winter sunset over Sunbiggin Tarn, a nature reserve owned by the Friends of the Lake District. Together with Great Asby Scar, itself a NNR, this SSSI is important for a wide variety of migrating birds.

Bluebells and beech trees at Lowther Park just beside the now derelict Lowther Castle. The woods at Lowther are an ancient deer park and still remain so, with a large herd of red deer free to roam behind protective deer fencing.

Late afternoon sun slants over Crookdale below the A6 over Shap Fell, a view that has been shared with hundreds of thousands of commercial drivers who have laboured up and down this famous fell road. Before the opening of the M6 motorway, this was the only route north and south between Kendal and Penrith and was often blocked by snowfall in winter time.

The M6 motorway snakes through the Lune Gorge at Tebay, past the Howgills where a Roman road took a similar route through the gorge. The M6 reaches its highest (and coldest) point at Shap summit – 320 metres above sea level. When it was opened in 1970, the motorway transformed communications through Cumbria with the resulting explosion in tourism and travel that we see today.

These red sandstone gargoyles and carved inscriptions are over a hundred years old at Armathwaite, overlooking the River Eden. Although beautifully carved, they are hidden away beside the river bank, seen only by those who go looking.

Shap Abbey, now in ruins and conserved by English Heritage, was built in 1199 and finally dissolved in 1540.

Bongate Mill at Appleby is a Georgian watermill beside the River Eden. Now the home of a writer and sculptor it houses a gallery and studio.

Colourful Little Salkeld Watermill is the only fully functional watermill in Cumbria and still produces stone-ground organic flours by water power.

Opposite
Built in 1762, the Eden Bridge crosses the River Eden at Lazonby.

Pendragon Castle at Mallerstang. In legend it was founded by Uther Pendragon, father of King Arthur – in reality it was probably built by Hugh de Morville in the twelfth century.

Kirkby Stephen Station was leased and restored by the Settle and Carlisle Railway Trust, which was formed when the famously scenic line was saved from closure in 1989. There is an exhibition relating to the Midland Railway Co, who built the line, housed within the station.

Curious folds of fields near Kirkby Stephen catch the low winter sun.

At Stenkrith Park, Kirkby Stephen, the River Eden powers through the viaduct arch and under the Millennium Bridge. A riverside walk follows its course with a sculture trail to admire along the way.

A footpath sign etched against early morning mist waymarks the Coast to Coast route over the Orton Fells from Hardendale.

Appleby's Low Cross seen from the Cloisters at the bottom of Boroughgate – described as one of finest streets in England.
Appleby is the county town of what was once Westmorland and even today, the history and atmosphere of the town is evident.
Of course most visitors will know Appleby for its historic gypsy Horse Fair, which has taken place in the town since 1685.

The stepping stones over the River Lowther at Shap, bathed in evening light, give way to the moorlands of the Shap Fells which provide a unique breeding environment for ground nesting birds during the spring.

The large market town of Penrith is steeped in history and still retains its traditional country charm in its red sandstone buildings – quite different from the limestone and slate of the central and southern Cumbrian towns.

Opposite
Long Meg and her Daughters is said to be the third biggest stone circle in the country. Sited near the village of Little Salkeld local folklore tells of a coven of witches celebrating their sabbath when a magician found them and turned them into stone. It's said that if the circle is moved or destroyed terrible misfortune will fall upon those responsible.

Walkers are well catered for in the Eden Valley with quiet dales and far-reaching views to make up for the lower heights of its fells and scars.

Brougham Castle is in ruins now, but a fort has existed on this site – just outside Penrith – since the Romans were here. What's left are the remains of the Clifford family's castle last occupied in 1676 when Lady Ann Clifford died here.

The Corus lime processing plant at junction 39, Shap, is a visible landmark for all travellers on the M6 motorway. The quarry that serves this plant forms a gaping hole in the landscape at Hardendale, just out of sight but the site's days may be numbered as the quarry nears the end of its productive life.

Alston is said to be the highest market town in England, at over 1000 feet above sea level. It's certainly remote, perched out on the eastern edge of Cumbria. In every direction, Alston is approached over the wild Pennine landscape which has been designated an Area of Outstanding Natural Beauty. Famous for its cheese, Alston has a steeply cobbled main street and a distinctive market cross dating from the seventeenth century.

Askham Village – one of the most sought after villages in the region – has changed remarkably little since it was planned by the Sandford family of Askham Hall in the thirteenth century. The settlement eventually became the property of the nearby Lowther estate and remains the quintessential Cumbrian village.

The Borders

The Cumbrian Borders region is something of an enigma. If you talk about the "Borders" people assume you mean the Scottish Borders; that you are addressing a Scottish region and Scottish locations; that you are referring to Scottish history. Hadrian drew a line in the soil here, to terminate the vast Roman Empire and the Border Wars came about because from 945 until 1070, Cumbria was ruled by Scottish kings and thereafter followed 700 years of conflict and local dispute across the border in equal measure. So it's not surprising that there exist, "two" Borders – the Scottish version and the English version. It's also no surprise that such a long period of turmoil has produced a trove of historical archaeology, architecture, fact and fiction. What is surprising is that apart from a few well marketed and easily packaged displays of history – the Wall, obviously, and Carlisle's more attractive monuments, the odd priory, church, fort or castle here and there – the greater part of the Border region of Cumbria remains largely unknown, un-exploited, un-marketed and to a greater or lesser extent wild.

Outside of the city of Carlisle and the narrow corridor of Hadrian's great defensive line there is little information and much less incentive to explore but for those who do, there is much to discover. The great historic sites are all easily accessible from Carlisle because the border region of Cumbria is essentially very narrow. Carlisle occupies the central position with Bowness-on-Solway bounding the west coast at the terminus of the Wall and Birdoswald Roman Fort and Gilsland straddling the Northumberland boundary to the east. Brampton and Longtown provide the only tangible destinations in between. To find the essence of the Border region you must search in the places in between. They are sparsely populated, remote and windswept places, scattered and timeless. Very different characters to the snug Lakeland villages we are all familiar with. The people are self sufficient, hardy and uncomplaining. The history is found in lonely memorials, abandoned ruins and ancient relics. They are still waiting to be found because they have been left alone. The landscape is not dramatic in scale but it is largely untouched and it has its own wild beauty. It's part of what makes Cumbria such a strange and compelling place.

Opposite
Wigton Market Cross Fountain
The ancient market town of Wigton, just ten miles from Carlisle lies on the Solway Plain between the Caldbeck Fells and the Solway Coast. The town was destroyed during a typically violent Scottish raid in 1322, but the pre-medieval street plan can still be traced today. The triangular market place stood at the centre of the town and where a wooden Market Cross once stood, a particularly ornate memorial fountain now stands proud – erected in 1872 by George Moore in memory of his wife. These days Wigton promotes itself as a "Literary" book town, being the birthplace of writer and broadcaster Melvyn Bragg.

Talkin Tarn

Talkin Tarn Country Park. This glacial tarn, formed about 10,000 years ago, is fed by underground streams and provides a tranquil setting for water sports and recreation for nearby Carlisle. In particular, rowing and fishing are popular with the resident rowing club holding an annual regatta each summer. An excellent café sits at the head of the tarn. Walks through the surrounding woodland are popular and there is a path round the tarn, which is always busy with families and dogs.

Bewcastle

Bewcastle and villages like this all along the wild Cumbrian/Scottish border were at the centre of the Scottish Reivers' many violent incursions into England during the thirteenth to the seventeenth centuries. There has been a fort of one sort or another here from the Romans onwards. The earliest construction was wood but in the thirteenth century a stone construction was begun. By the fifteenth century it had begun to decay but under Richard, Duke of Gloucester (later King Richard III), who became Warden of the West March, repairs were made. This lawless period for the Borders meant that castles such as this and the nearby Askerton and Naworth would have provided sanctuary for the locals during raids by the Scots. A leaflet about the castle is available from Demesne Farm next door.

St Cuthbert's church and the Bewcastle Cross

Along with the castle itself, Bewcastle treasures its seventh century cross, standing tall in the church yard, though missing the cross-piece. The pillar is carved with runic symbols, the meaning of which is lost in history but this cross has stood in this original position since the late 600s when this region was still known as Rheged. It has seen the changing fortunes of the Border region, once under Northumbrian sway, surviving the violence of the feuding reivers and the rebuilding of the church several times.

Opposite

Bank's Turret, Hadrian's Wall

The western section of Hadrian's Wall went from Bowness-on-Solway, on the west coast, to the River Irthing near Harrow's Scar. It was first built of turf, with stone turrets but within ten years the turf wall was replaced with stone and the turrets were incorporated into the stone wall. At Bank's Turret (Turret 52A) the turret still remains along with a short stretch of wall that runs alongside the quiet road. It seems odd to think of the history tied up in these old walls lying peacefully at the roadside, un-remarked save for an occasional information board or footpath sign. The wall is a reminder that Cumbria has been at the wild edge of more than one empire down through the ages.

Birdoswald Roman Fort

Birdoswald remains the best-preserved of any Wall fort and stands above a meander in the River Irthing. Birdoswald is one of the most scenic settings along Hadrian's Wall and a Roman fort, turret and milecastle are all visible along this stretch. Today Birdoswald is a popular visitor attraction and interpretation centre but in the past it has served as a fortified farm house and stronghold from the infamous Border Reivers.

Brampton Moot Hall

Brampton is another ancient market town, so typical of Cumbria's outer edges. It has been here since the seventh century and the mark of history is all around. The octagonal Moot Hall, built in 1817 by the Earl of Lancaster, has centre stage in the cobbled market place. Once the setting for a poultry, eggs and butter market, it now houses the Tourist Information Centre. The building stands on the site of an earlier one from 1648, once used by Cromwell to house prisoners and a ring post in front of the Moot Hall recalls the ancient "sport" of bull baiting. Brampton has plenty of history and legend to occupy the curious and is worth exploring.

Lannercost Priory

Lannercost Priory holds the distinction of being the last of the great Augustinian priories to be founded (in 1166) and the last to be dissolved, by Henry VIII in 1536. When completed in 1220, canons came from the priory in Norfolk, and remained for 370 years until the Dissolution of the Monasteries. Eventually the building was given to Thomas Dacre of nearby Naworth Castle who converted some of the structure into Dacre Hall. In around 1740 it was decided to restore the nave, and use it as a parish church which thankfully has resulted in the survival of a large part of the building in its full height and splendour.

Carlisle Castle

When you stand before the squat and resolute fortress of Carlisle Castle you are looking at 900 years of turmoil, invasion, misery and war. Carlisle has always born the brunt of the violence waged between Scotland and England – indeed when the castle was built on the orders of William II, son of William the Conquerer, Cumberland was considered part of Scotland and the Scots were not easily ejected! Over the centuries this fortress has seen a lot of action and changed hands many times. In 1648 Mary Queen of Scots was imprisoned here, as were many from the Jacobite army of 1745. Even up until 1959 it was the home of the Border Regiment. Now it remains as testimony and museum to all of this history and has lost none of its presence and resilience.

Carlisle Guildhall Museum

Carlisle's Guildhall Museum is housed in a medieval building, just behind the Market Place and Tourist Information centre. In 1382 a fire destroyed much of Carlisle leaving this site to be rebuilt into a home in 1405 by Richard of Redeness. When he died he left his home to Carlisle city and it became the Guildhall for the city's trade guilds. The timber-framed construction is in-filled with thin medieval tile bricks with internal walls made from inter-woven twigs with a covering of clay. Now the building houses a museum relating to the trades guilds and history of the city including stocks used for punishing criminals, the chest which kept the city's valuables safe in the Middle Ages and other artefacts.

The Borders from Talkin

With no more high fells to interrupt the view, a big sky dominates the flat expanse of border country north of Brampton. This is where Hadrian pushed his wall across the north and generations of Border "Reiver" families north and south of the Scottish border fought bitter land disputes and rustled cattle.

Opposite

Haining Burn, Midgeholme – the Cumbrian border

This remote corner, where the Alston to Brampton road crosses and re-crosses the Northumbria/Cumbria border is as far east as you can go in northern Cumbria, though Alston itself is further east. These are the north Pennines and the Pennine Way lies just over the ridge just a mile or two away. The Lake District fells might well be in another county – indeed they nearly are!

Farmland at Castle Carrock

A typical north Pennine village, Castle Carrock is a farming community at heart. Surrounded by fertile land and low fells with far reaching views, these northern villages are charming but rugged – hard working and down to earth. Even so, the Weary Sportsman is a successful, and very contemporary restaurant that has won the Cumbrian Restaurant of the Year award – a surprise for the visitor but typical of rural Cumbria.

The Weary Sportsman

Kershope Forest
Kershope is part of the vast Keilder Forest group that straddles the English/Scottish border from the edge of Cumbria across Northumberland. The famous RAC rally used to run stages through here but for most of the year the only sounds heard will be the buzz of chainsaws as the Forestry Commission harvest timber.

West Cumbria

A relatively small percentage of visitors to Cumbria venture further west than Borrowdale in the north and Coniston in the south and to both visitors and local Cumbrians, living in and around the Lakeland heartland, West Cumbria can seem a long way away. For many, it is a long way away – an hour and a half's drive from Kendal or Penrith. This isolation has been a blessing and a curse in many ways but it has forced towns and villages along the Cumbrian coastline to forge a fiercely independent life and to turn to the resources at hand to grow and prosper. Industry, shipping, trade and commerce have been the lifeblood of the coast since the industrial revolution. Barrow-in-Furness exploited its unique deep water harbour and rose to become, for a time, the greatest iron and steel producer in the world with ship building at its centre. It still has the largest ship building halls in Europe!

Whitehaven too, has a glorious industrial and commercial history. From the seventeenth century onwards Whitehaven became a major centre for coal exports, silk and rum. It saw the first ever under-sea coal-mine shaft in the world, an amazing achievement in its day. The town was one of the very first planned Georgian towns in the country – built to a design by Sir Christopher Wren – and has over 250 listed buildings. Workington, just up the coast has a similar story – iron and steel manufacture have long been a part of Workington's heritage, and it was here that the famous Henry Bessemer first introduced his revolutionary steel making process. Now, with the decline of the steel industry and coal mining, the town has diversified into other forms of industry and steel making is no longer a part of life here. In fact heavy industry on the West coast of Cumbria has all but vanished. Even Sellafield, a former Second World War munitions factory, which became Britain's first nuclear complex in the late 1940s, is now being decommissioned.

However, in place of all this industry and trade, we are discovering again the natural beauty of an environment that was here all the time but overlooked. The Victorians knew about it. They established spa resorts on the coast to savour the bracing sea air and salt water – Silloth, Allonby and Maryport all expanded with the coming of the railways and the Victorian tourists, and now their time is coming again. Regeneration, rebuilding and re-discovery – it's happening up and down the West Cumbrian coast. The region boasts bird reserves, protected coastal and estuary environments and quiet, empty, sandy beaches that are internationally important and as good as anywhere in the country. It's a wonder that West Cumbria remains as quiet as it does.

Opposite
St Bees, Fleswick Bay
In between StBees Head to the north and St Bees beach and village to the south lies Fleswick Bay, a half moon of shingle and sand with sculpted sandstone slabs and layered cliffs. A footpath snakes down a narrow gully at the north end to give access to one of the most beautifully secluded and atmospheric locations anywhere in Cumbria. Relaxing and idyllic on a calm summer's day it can be equally inspiring when wave-lashed and battered by winter gales and you can be sure of a quiet time – access is by foot or boat only.

The Solway Firth from Bowness-on-Solway

Cumbria's west coast is topped and tailed by two of the most remarkable natural habitats in Europe: Morecambe Bay to the south and the Solway Firth in the north. Of the two, the Solway is more remote, isolated and untouched. There are no large centres of population here – indeed barely anyone lives here at all – just a few scattered hamlets and farms, utilising the salt marshes for sheep and cattle. This wild landscape, largely overlooked by visitors, is one of the treasures of West Cumbria.

Defence of the Harbour statue

There's a great deal of industrial and maritime history associated with the Georgian town of Whitehaven but its most curious connection is with the "invasion" by the American Navy of 1778 during the War of Independence. Led by John Paul Jones, a Scot who sailed from Whitehaven in his youth, the fledgling American Navy attempted to burn the harbour and its fleet but were waylaid in the local pub and got drunk instead! The American Navy has since been granted the freedom of the harbour and has visited during the Whitehaven Maritime Festival along with other stunning examples of original and reconstructed tall ships, like the *Grand Turk*. The history of the harbour and its defense are illustrated by a number of sculptures like this one which shows a canon being used to fend off attacks. The town also has a long history of both trade and smuggling – vividly brought to life at the Rum Story museum.

Above
The kinetic clock at the Rum Story museum

The *Grand Turk* at Whitehaven Maritime Festival

Herring gulls perched at St Bees Head

St Bees Head, a towering – or perhaps tottering – cliff of red sandstone is home to the largest seabird colony in north-west England. Guillemots, kittiwakes, fulmars and razorbills wheel overhead, while ravens and peregrines can often be seen hunting along the cliffs. Out to sea skuas and shearwaters might be skimming the surf, you may even spot dolphins and porpoises. The herring gull population seem to be the noisiest and most common seabirds here, easily observed from one of three RSPB viewing points along the spectacular sea cliff walk.

St Bees Head

St Bees is the only heritage coast between Anglesey and the Scottish border. In fact it is the only sea cliff in between. The striking red sandstone reaches some 300 feet high and affords excellent views north to Scotland and across to the Isle of Man on a clear day.
St Bees is named after St Bega, a seventh-century Irish saint who founded a priory here. The Cumbria Coastal Way runs along the cliff-top path, past a dazzling white lighthouse and on to Whitehaven.

St Bees beach

For most visitors to St Bees it will be the historic little village and friendly beach that will be the first they see of this coastline. The beach at low tide is sandy and popular with families in the summer and for the adventurous, a scramble around on the red sandstone rocks and slabs beneath the cliffs will reveal a real surprise: dozens of carvings and engravings, beautifully executed, some over two hundred years old – graffiti carved in the soft rock so many years ago and still visible today.

Drigg sand dunes

Drigg has a split personality. To the immediate north and within sight, is Sellafield nuclear power station. Drigg is the site of the UK's national low-level radioactive waste repository. Although there's little evidence of much radioactive waste actually being buried there, there are stories of a fire engine and even a bus buried in the trenches. And yet only a short distance away is beautiful, secluded Drigg beach. A SSSI with marram grass-covered sand dunes stretching away to the estuary of the River Esk, known as Eskmeals and Black Combe squatting on the horizon. It's difficult to overlook Sellafield but easy to enjoy the beach.

Allonby beach

Designated an Area of Outstanding Natural Beauty, Allonby once enjoyed fame as a Victorian health resort and is still a favourite destination for many beach goers. Situated on the north west coast of Cumbria between Mayport and Silloth, the tides of the Solway Firth recede for over half a mile leaving clean, soft sand on which to enjoy just about any beach activity you like. Windsurfing and kite surfing are particularly popular.

Ravenglass & "L'al Ratty" Ravenglass and Eskdale Steam Railway

Ravenglass is another tiny Cumbrian coastal village that punches well above its weight! It lies within the Lake District National Park on the estuary of three rivers – the Esk, the Mite and the Irt and was known to be an important Roman naval base in the second century, known as Glannaventa. Only the remains of a Roman bath house offer clues to this past. Industry was here too. Iron ore, granite and copper ore were brought to the estuary by narrow gauge railway from mines in Eskdale and the line has been preserved – "L'al Ratty" as the Ravenglass and Eskdale Steam Railway is affectionately known carries passengers up and down all summer long. Only a mile or so away is Muncaster Castle with its splendid ornamental gardens and famous World Owl Trust.

Shrimp boat on the Solway Firth off Silloth

The Solway shrimping fleet is not what it once was but then again the multiple conservation designations of the area reflect the environmental importance of the Solway. The inner Solway estuary is a Special Protection Area (SPA), Special Area of Conservation (SAC) and Site of Special Scientific Interest (SSSI). Wigtown Bay in the outer Solway comprises the UK's largest Local Nature Reserve all of which has come about because over-fishing in the 1990s just about emptied the Solway of shellfish. The fishing grounds have re-opened on a limited basis and the stocks are recovering slowly. Both the Solway and Morecambe Bay are more environmentally diverse and endangered than the entire Lake District National Park.

Silloth-on-Solway

Like the fishing industry, Silloth itself has seen more prosperous times, but it is bouncing back, slowly. Situated south of Carlisle the town is actually very handsome with wide cobbled avenues and grand buildings that recall its Victorian heyday as a spa resort.

Maryport harbour

Maryport is another West Cumbrian harbour town with an historic past – from the Romans onwards. This delightful harbour-side town situated on the Solway Firth boasts a Roman fort, Georgian buildings, Victorian docks, and industries, which have included coal mining, iron making, shipping and shipbuilding. Recently, regeneration grants have seen the development of a new marina and the town is becoming more and more popular with visitors.

Black Combe from Silecroft beach
Silecroft is where the mountains of the Lake District meet the sea. Black Combe is a popular fell walk with far reaching views whilst Silecroft lies on the Cumbria Coastal Way. Silecroft itself once thrived producing salt from sea-water evaporation but now it lies well off the tourists' radar even though the beach offers miles of uninterrupted sand at low tide.

Silecroft sunset

Drift wood log on Silecroft beach
Beach combing, walking the dog, summer evening barbeques, salt
wind in your hair – the Cumbrian coast does seem a long way away
from it all and remains for the most part a backwater to be explored
and enjoyed.

Furness Abbey, Barrow-in-Furness

Furness Abbey was one of the richest Cistercian monasteries in England, second only to Fountains Abbey in Yorkshire. Only the ruins of the red sandstone buttresses and arches remain of this 700 year old site but they speak of the wealth and importance that Barrow once had.

Barrow Docks and the Dock Museum

Barrow-in-Furness has not enjoyed prosperity for some time now, but consider this – in the mid 1800s it grew from a tiny fishing hamlet to the biggest iron and steel centre in the world, and a major ship-building centre. The railway carried iron-ore, slate and limestone to the new deep water port and its prosperity grew with the development of the steel and ship-building industries. Today, the town still relies on naval contracts. In fact the ship building hall is the largest in Europe. Its heyday is gone though not forgotten. The new, modern Dock Museum highlights the past whilst developments aimed at regenerating the dock area as a tourist destination have brought a new lease of life to the town.

Piel Castle from Walney Island

The castle on Piel Island stands as a fortified house guarding the entrance to Barrow's deep water harbour. Constructed before 1372, when Edward III granted leave to fortify the existing building to the Abbot of Furness Abbey the castle is now in the hands of English Heritage and can be reached by ferry from nearby Roa Island.

Walney Island nature reserve and lighthouse

Walney Island's south nature reserve is said to be the biggest gullery in Europe with 17,000 pairs of Lesser Black Back and Herring Gulls, two of Britain's largest species. The reserve is managed by Cumbria Wildlife Trust and offers visitors a network of footpaths amongst the sand dunes with information boards and hides from which to bird-watch. The contrast out here, from the busy, industrial streets of Barrow to this remote-feeling oasis of peace and solace is remarkable.

Walney Island nature reserve and lighthouse

Lake District

The Lake District National Park is a complex and contradictory place. The way it looks, the way it works and the precarious balancing act that its traditions, industries, ecology and people maintain against the ever-more powerful forces of change and modernisation are constantly tested. But then again they always have been. Ever since William Wordsworth published his *Guide Through the District of the Lakes* in 1820, the Lake District has been a magnet for visitors that gave rise to an explosion of development and change, to service the Victorian masses arriving on the newly-built railways.

This small cartwheel of upland mountains and fells, lakes, tarns and villages was in mortal danger from the millions who came to rejoice, explore and ultimately exploit it. The very thing that drew the crowds to the most northern, rugged, mountainous, wettest region in England – the Lake District's astonishing natural beauty – would be its undoing. The Lake District National Park, designated in 1951 as England's first and largest national park, recognised that something had to be done. Conservation, management and development to meet the conflicting needs of the visiting and visited has been going on ever since. Tourism is responsible for over 50% of Cumbria's income and over 50% of Cumbria's jobs servicing 12 million visitors a year.

The Lake District as we see it today is not a museum piece, preserved from an idealised past, it's still in constant flux and development. Neither is it a particularly natural environment. The landscape is heavily managed, maintained and controlled. Planning regulations say just what can and cannot be built, what it must look like, how it must conform and fit into a Lakeland sense of identity. Conservation in the Lakes is a multi-million pound industry. Hill farming, once taken for granted in this rural district, is no longer profitable but the hill farms must be maintained to keep the look of the place, to manage the land. Indeed it is the hill farms that largely shaped the way the Lakes look today. Sheep so overgrazed the fells in the past that all the once heavily wooded, lower valleys are now bare of trees. Charcoal burning, bobbin mills, quarrying and mining scarred and exploited the fells and valleys for over 500 years. Now only a few operations are left scratching a living, barely registering on most visitors' radar. In place of these age-old industries and livelihoods comes tourism and recreation. Walking, climbing, sailing, pottering, motoring around, sightseeing and shopping. The activities that take place within the National Park both define it and shape it.

Opposite

Winter sunset over Kentmere
The Kentmere Valley, accessed from the little village of Staveley, lies between Windermere and Kendal. Whilst the single-track road terminates in a scattered settlement of traditional houses, farms and a church, the valley itself continues to a large reservoir fed by the source of the River Kent, surrounded by a high cirque of fells known as the Kentmere Horseshoe, one of the finest, high level horseshoe walks in the Lakes.

But there is one constant, one thing that has not, and does not change. The overwhelming, magical, almost fictional beauty of the landscape remains. That blend of water, fell, crag and summit, decorated with the white splashes of farm houses and barns, and the scribed lines of stone walls and sheep shelters seen reflected in the mirror of a perfectly still lake on a summer's morning, is still something that makes you stop in your tracks and take a deep breath. So the Lake District remains the jewel in Cumbria's crown.

Castlerigg at sunrise

Cyclist at Castlerigg stone circle
Castlerigg stone circle, sited atop a small hill but with impressive views of the Helvellyn range, Blencathra and Skiddaw, is one of the most important Neolithic sites in Britain. There are 38 stones in a circle approximately 30 metres wide. Within the ring, a rectangle of 10 standing stones, the tallest 2.3 metres high, have been laid. It was probably built around 3000 BC and is one of the earliest stone circles in Britain.

Cyclist climbing Hardknott Pass

Hardknott Pass, the ancient pack horse route that links the Duddon Valley with Eskdale, has always been a grueling ascent. No more so than as part of the annual Fred Whitton Challenge, in which cyclists complete a round of the six major Lakeland passes, 112 miles, in a charity ride. The fastest (and fittest) riders can complete the round in just over six hours!

Striding Edge in full winter conditions

Striding Edge, the knife-edge arête that scrambles up the south-eastern flank of Helvellyn, is probably the most famous ridge walk in England and presents a serious challenge in full winter conditions. For summer walkers unused to winter climbing in the Lake District, Striding Edge is best avoided in snow but for the more experienced and well equipped, a round of Helvellyn's Striding and Swirrel Edges will present a truly memorable day out.

Scafell Crag after a clearing, summer storm

Scafell (traditionally pronounced Scawfell) was considered to be higher than its neighbour, Scafell Pike, just the other side of the low saddle of Mickledore. Now we know that the Pike is not only the higher of the two but is the highest place in England – 3162 feet, or 964 metres if you prefer. But it was not the peaks that attracted the early pioneering rock climbers, it was this vast, imposing crag and its massive "Central Buttress", finally climbed in 1914 by Siegfried Herford and companions. It's still a daunting place for walkers and climbers alike, particularly in poor weather.

Napes Needle, Great Gable

In June of 1886, Walter Parry Haskett-Smith scrambled up to the base of this detached rock needle, from his holiday base at the Wasdale Head Inn, scanned its cracked and fissured features and made up his mind. He would climb it, solo. And in doing so, heralded the start of the modern sport of rock climbing, or so it goes. I was amused, though not altogether surprised to find a modern pair of climbers, recreating the Edwardian era for their own ascent in 2008, complete with flat hat, tweeds and Norfolk jackets, though not nailed boots and not solo. Such is the nostalgia, fame and affection in which this climb is held.

Needle Ridge, Great Gable

Immediately behind the Needle is a steep and narrow ridge line – Needle Ridge – which has become one of the finest low grade ridge climbs in the Lakes not least because of the spectacular airy views of the Wasdale Valley below. Being a mountain route, the weather will always add an element of the unpredictable.

Paddlers canoeing on Windermere

Windermere offers opportunities for water sports of all kinds although now that a 10mph speed limit has been controversially imposed, water skiing and jet skis have been severely curtailed. However, that has brought a level of peace and tranquillity to the lake, something enjoyed by sailors and paddlers.

Rowing boat on Grasmere

Grasmere has always been a haven of peace and tranquillity, enjoyed via traditional Lakeland rowing boats since Wordsworths' day. The Lakeland rowing boat is a unique design. Long, heavy and clinker-built, these wooden boats used pintles rather than rowlocks for the oars and nearly every house with a lake frontage had one, often employed for towing spinners for pike. Nowadays, they can be hired on many of the popular lakes for a lazy cruise out on the water, though the modern, moulded plastic boats don't seem quite right.

Winter frost on rowing boats

Opposite
The Lakeside and Haverthwaite Steam Railway

The Lakeside and Haverthwaite Steam Railway, run by enthusiasts, is a short section of the former Furness line and runs between Lakeside at the foot of Windermere and Haverthwaite where the company has its railway yard. This popular attraction still ferries passengers to catch the steamers from the old Victorian pier at Lakeside and for train buffs, the railway's locomotive fleet includes FR 0-4-0 No. 20, the oldest, working, standard gauge steam loco in Britain, built in 1863.

The Britannia Inn, Elterwater, Great Langdale

For many, the perfect Lakeland day out will include lunch at a country pub and the "Brit" as it's known locally, is as quintessential as it comes. This 400 year old, former "gentleman farmer's residence" sits on the green in the tiny hamlet of Elterwater, in the heart of Great Langdale. There are few more congenial places to spend a sunny afternoon after a good morning's walk.

Derwent Water and Skiddaw

Borrowdale is home to the busy town of Keswick, the tranquil lake of Derwent Water and the massive bulk of Skiddaw, all of which can be viewed via an easily accessible and very pleasant fell – Catbells. Derwent Water is 3 miles long and about 1 mile wide but shallow so it warms quickly in summer and freezes over readily in the winter. Skiddaw is one of the Lake's four "3000'ers" – that is mountains over 3000ft – the others being Scafell Pike, Scafell and Helvellyn.

Bassenthwaite Lake and Skiddaw

Bassenthwaite Lake lies to the north-west of Keswick and has a number of unique qualities; It's the shallowest lake in the district at only 70 feet deep but is one of the longest at 4 miles. It is the most northern of all the lakes and is home to a most rare species of fish, the Vendace (Coregonus albula), found in Britain only here and in neighbouring Derwent Water. But more curious than that, Bassenthwaite Lake is the only "Lake" in the Lake District. All the others are "Meres" and "Waters".

Bassenthwaite Lake

Skiddaw and Blencathra at Threlkeld

An ancient pack horse route winds up between the meeting of these two great fells, following the beck into what is known as Skiddaw Forest, ultimately arriving at an old hunting lodge, now a private hostel for walkers – Skiddaw House. There are no trees in Skiddaw Forest, there never were. "Forest" is an ancient term that described land that was used for hunting, often of course in woodland which is how the term has come to have its modern usage. Skiddaw House was built in the early 1800s as a keeper's cottage for grouse shooting but it was quarried slate that Skiddaw and the village of Threlkeld really thrived on.

Back O'Skiddaw – Barkbethdale

The northern flanks of Skiddaw offer a more remote and to many, a more interesting aspect than the usual view from Keswick and Borrowdale. Hill farming replaces hill walking to a large extent but for those prepared to explore these quiet valleys and lonely footpaths overlooking Bassenthwaite, the extra effort will be well rewarded and it's certainly the place to get away from it all.

Blencathra

The great saddleback of Blencathra lies immediately to the east of Skiddaw, overlooking the quarry village of Threlkeld, beside the busy A66 road. It dominates the skyline for drivers heading towards Keswick from Penrith and the M6 motorway, often clad in a mantle of snow during winter months or gathering storm clouds about its dished twin summits. The main attraction for the adventurous scrambler is a round of Sharp Edge and Halls Fell Ridge – up one and down the other – one of the most exposed outings in the Lake District.

Moonrise over Little Man and Skiddaw, from Keswick

Winter often brings periods of settled, high-pressure weather to the Lake District, with clear, sharp days and icy nights. A full, bright moon, rising over the fells late in the afternoon is too good an opportunity to miss and on this occasion I hurriedly pulled off the road, sprinted up a nearby hill and took aim, praying I would get there before the moon cleared the summit of Skiddaw's "Little Man".

Catbells from Friars Crag, Derwent Water

The popular viewpoint of Friars Crag, a short walk from the Keswick landing stages, offers a front row seat overlooking some of the most classically beautiful scenery to be found in Britain. On any clear, still morning photographers gather to capture the sun seeping over the sharply defined ridge of Catbells, across the bay and more often than not gather a few images of the rowing boats, dragged up on the shingle for the night. Well trodden footpaths guide visitors past a bronze memorial to the Victorian reformer John Ruskin and around a short circuit of well chosen viewpoints, with benches overlooking a half moon beach of grass and shingle towards Lords Island, with its ruined manor house now vanished into the undergrowth. The house was once the residence of the Earls of Derwentwater and had a drawbridge over the water but the earldom was forfeit after the Jacobite rising of 1715.

Derwent Water at Friars Crag

Derwent Water and Lords Island

Autumn colours at Brandlehow Bay

Opposite
Brandlehow Bay, Derwent Water
There can be few more perfect locations in which to live! Brandlehow Bay lies at the end of a scenic footpath around the shores of Derwent Water with easy access and stunning views across the lake, and a series of interesting art works and sculptures installed along the water's edge. For many, the autumn months offer the most rewarding sights as the multitude of deciduous trees throughout Borrowdale display their colours.

Ashness Bridge, Borrowdale

It is often quoted that the little packhorse bridge at Ashness, on the Watendlath road is the most photographed scene in the whole of the Lake District. It wouldn't surprise me. This scene has been a subject of landscape photographers almost since the birth of photography with some fine images taken from 1880 onwards. Viewing those old pictures, it's striking how little the scene has changed. The trees are taller and the road has been surfaced but otherwise it is unaltered in over a hundred years.

Stockley Bridge, Borrowdale

Walkers heading up the hill to Great Gable, Scafell or over Sty Head Pass to Wasdale, will pass over this ancient packhorse bridge just as countless travellers have done for hundreds of years, for many of these traditional bridges have survived for centuries. The passes were natural trading routes between valleys and dales that would otherwise take a full day's travel to reach and packhorses provided the transport. The mountain streams – "becks" – run clear and cold with run-off directly from the fells and swell dramatically after rain.

Details of Stockley Beck

Sty Head Tarn and Great End

Linking Borrowdale with Wasdale, Sty Head Pass and its little diamond shaped tarn, provide the perfect resting place for tired walkers at the end of the day and see a fair number of mountain campers looking for a memorable night out under the stars. The mound of Great End gives way to a sheer cliff of buttresses and deep gullies on its northern side, which has made it a favourite venue for winter climbers when snow and ice cover these high central fells.

Ritson's Force, Wasdale Head

The Wasdale Valley lays claim to a number of boasts – it has the highest summit in England, Scafell Pike, the deepest lake, Wastwater, the smallest church – St Olaf's – and the biggest liar! Will Ritson was the landlord of the Wasdale Head Inn in the late 1800s and had a reputation for story telling that lives on to this day in the form of the Biggest Liar in the World Competition, held annually in the valley. This secluded waterfall and cold, clear pool is known as Ritson's Force in memory of this great local character.

Buttermere with Fleetwith Pike and High Crag

Buttermere and Crummock Water lie over the Honest Pass from Borrowdale and remain mostly untouched by the majority of visitors to the Lake District although walkers make the effort in droves. Indeed the doyen of all fell walkers, Alfred Wainwright, chose Hay Stack above Buttermere as the place for his ashes to be scattered.

Loweswater and Mellbreak

Loweswater might well be the most overlooked of all the lakes in the district. Tucked away beyond Crummock Water, to which it was once joined, Loweswater enjoys a peaceful existence away from the crowds, explored by relatively few.

Ennerdale Water

Ennerdale is the most westerly of the lakes and serves as a reservoir for nearby West Cumbrian towns. Much of the land is owned by the Forestry Commission. Sadly the valley floor has been largely exploited for soft wood timber. There is no road around the lake – indeed the car park that exists brings the few walkers and sightseers who make the journey only to the lake foot – after that you are on your own. In spite of this, there exists one of the most remote Youth Hostels in the country at the head of Ennerdale. Under the shadow of Great Gable, Black Sail Hostel is a former shepherd's bothy with no frills – it has become something of a legend amongst Coast-to-Coast walkers who stay here.

Hardknott Pass and Roman fort

The famously steep, switchback fell road of Hardknott Pass has been in use for centuries. The Romans built a defensive fort here, looking out over Eskdale towards the distant coastline at Ravenglass (Glannaventa). Built between AD120 and AD138 during the reign of Emperor Hadrian, Hardknott Fort (Mediobogdum) is one of finest Roman forts still visible in the country.

Cockley Beck Bridge and the River Duddon
The Duddon Valley is a remote and sometimes overlooked valley, that lies between the famous passes of Wrynose and Hardknott. At Cockley Beck, drivers make a sharp right turn over the old packhorse bridge and prepare for the hairpin corners of Hardknott but the river valley is stunningly beautiful, particularly beneath autumn colours and it is only its remoteness that has kept it quiet and unspoiled.

The Langdale Pikes from Tarn Hows

Opposite page:
The Langdale Pikes from Easthwaite, near Hawkshead
The Langdale Pikes are probably the most instantly recognisable
mountain profile in the Lake District and perhaps Langdale itself the
most popular valley. The "Long Dale' is indeed a long valley – over 4
miles along the valley floor. Langdale has been a magnet for walkers,
climbers and outdoor lovers since the Victorian era and yet it has
remained largely unchanged and free from development even though
during the peak season it fills to bursting with visitors.

Loughrigg Tarn, Great Langdale
Loughrigg Tarn is one of several tarns that dot the landscape
throughout the Langdale Valley. Beautifully proportioned and ideally
situated beside a quiet fell road, Wordsworth considered it a favourite
place and described it as "round, clear and bright as heaven".

Wetherlam from Elterwater, Great Langdale

From a distance Wetherlam stands proudly aloof, overlooking the Langdale Valley at its feet. But up close its true nature is revealed, for this fell is the most industrialised of any of the Lake Districts mountains – from copper mining to slate quarrying, workings and spoil tips litter its face. Elterwater was a base for a gunpowder works (now the Langdales hotel) to feed the mines and copper was extracted in huge quantities up until the late 1800s, with some shafts plunging to over 700 ft deep. The south side of this massif overlooks Coniston and was extensively mined – today it is known as Coppermines Valley.

Coniston Water, landing stage at Brantwood

Brantwood House and the steam ship, *Gondola* on Coniston Water
John Ruskin, poet, artist, critic, social revolutionary and conservationist, a towering figure of the Victorian era, settled in Coniston in 1871. He'd been a devoted visitor to the Lakes from childhood, and soon set about renovating and landscaping the grounds into the fine country house that now attracts visitors from around the world. The *Gondola* steam yacht is the oldest steam yacht in the North of England and was built in 1859 by the Furness Railway Company as an attraction for tourists travelling up to Coniston by train. It was abandoned in 1960 but rescued by the National Trust, rebuilt at Vickers in Barrow and re-launched on Coniston in 1980. And, of course, Coniston is remembered for Donald Campbell's fatal attempt at the world water speed record in *Bluebird*. It was 8.55 on the morning of the 4th January 1967 when he hit a floating log and lost control. *Bluebird* has been resurrected and will eventually be housed in Coniston village.

Tarn Hows, Coniston

Often cited as the most visited beauty spot in the Lake District, Tarn Hows is situated in a natural hollow on the summit of Hawkshead Hill, with fine views over the surrounding fells and footpaths to direct visitors around the shoreline. It is not, however, an entirely natural scene, for originally there were three, shallow, interconnecting tarns surrounded by a marshy wetland. In 1862, the landowner, a wealthy industrialist James Garth Marshall succumbed to the Victorian preference for landscaped and engineered scenery and flooded the tarns to create a small lake, planted specimen trees – conifers mostly – and declared it a beauty spot! It was eventually bought by Beatrix Potter in the 1930s, who transferred it to the National Trust.

High Dam, Finsthwaite, near Lakeside

At the southern end of Windermere near Lakeside, stands a working industrial relic – Stott Park Bobbin Mill. The industrial age of the Lancashire cotton mills demanded huge quantities of bobbins on which to wind cotton thread and the abundance of cheap water power in the Lake District saw the rise of a great many bobbin mills, turning larch poles into bobbins by the thousand and water mills needed reservoirs. High Dam was constructed to supply Stott Park, just down the hill, with a constant source of water. The legacy of this industrial operation is a wonderfully peaceful and tranquil series of still lakes – reservoirs – set in woodland, the raw material for the mill.

Windermere steamer heading home in the evening, from Brant Fell

Windermere steamer, first sailing on a still morning from Storrs Hall

Opposite

Windermere from Brant Fell

Brant Fell is a small outlook above Bowness-on-Windermere that offers one of the best viewpoints over the lake, particularly as the sun declines in the west, late in the day. From here the whole length of England's largest lake is just about visible. To the north is Ambleside, the Langdale Pikes and the mass of the Fairfield Horseshoe. Across the lake to the west lie the fells of Coniston and to the south, Morecambe Bay. The most persistent presence on the 10 ½ mile stretch of water are the water buses and the splendid iron steamers – no longer steam powered of course – which were built in the 1930s. Steamers have operated on the lake since 1845 when the first steam boat, a paddle steamer named *Lady of The Lake* was launched – with considerable opposition from, amongst others, William Wordsworth.

Sunset over Windermere from Brant Fell

Troutbeck

Troutbeck village perched along a steep sided valley, has retained its traditional look and feel through the ages. The Kirkstone Pass coach road, which now by-passes the village, was an important link for villagers and there remain a number of unique features here: a traditional yeoman farmer's residence, preserved by the National Trust, an old coaching inn, the Queen's Head with its famous bar constructed from an Elizabethan four poster bed, and the farm once owned by Beatrix Potter, also now a National Trust property, are all here.

The Kirkstone Pass Inn

Kirkstone Pass is the highest road pass in the Lakes at 1489 feet. The climb from Ambleside is 1 in 4 in places and is aptly named "the struggle". The Kirkstone Pass Inn is actually the third highest pub in the country and is particularly busy when snow covers the fells because if the pass is drivable this is a very popular destination. The name "Kirkstone" is derived from a strikingly shaped boulder beside the road that is said to resemble a little chapel.

Bridge House, Ambleside

Bridge House may be the most photographed building in the Lake District. It was certainly popular with artists, including Turner. Built originally as an apple store for nearby Ambleside Hall, it was constructed over Stock Beck to escape land tax. Now it houses the National Trust Information Centre in Ambleside, who probably wish they had opted for more space as Ambleside continues to expand and thrive with ever more visitors crowding its narrow lanes. It was the railways and the lake steamers that were largely responsible for Ambleside's success as the Victorians built the town up into the tourist centre it has become.

Rydal Hall summer house

Away from Ambleside, nearby Rydal is a much calmer location and walkers can enjoy a very pleasant walk around the shoreline footpath, admiring the waterfowl and flocks of Canada geese that regularly gather here. Rydal Water, along with Grasmere, is of course the seat of the romantic poets led by William Wordsworth. He lived first at Dove Cottage, in Grasmere and then at Rydal Mount close by Rydal Water, where he often used the little summer house beside the beck to write his verse.

Rydal Water

Grasmere

Grasmere empties into Rydal Water and the two lakes share a common atmosphere of peace and tranquillity, no more so than on still, winter mornings with frost etching the shoreline. It seems impossible to mention Grasmere without reference to Wordsworth. He and his family are buried at St Oswald's church in the village – a grave that has become one of the most visited literary shrines in the world.

Helm Crag reflected in Grasmere

St Oswald's church, Grasmere

Brothers Water and the Kirkstone Pass

The descent from Kirkstone Pass northwards, leads steeply down into Patterdale with Brothers Water tucked into the valley bottom overshadowed by Red Screes and the twin valleys of Dovedale and Deepdale. Fewer tourists make the journey over the pass to this side of the lakes and the Ullswater Valley has a entirely different atmosphere to its busy sister, Windermere, even though Ullswater is the second largest lake.

Norfolk Island on a dark winter's day

Place Fell, opposite Glenridding on Ullswater

Ullswater is the second largest lake in the Lake District at 7 ½ miles long with two dog legs. Its serpentine course is largely undeveloped with only two small villages, one at either end, to attract the crowds. Glenridding sits at the south end, Pooley Bridge at the north, neither of them has access to a rail link or even much of a road and they have remained brisk but un-crowded. The east shore has a minor road that eventually ends in the remote and beautiful valley of Martindale and does not encircle the lake. To the west, dominating the skyline is mighty Helvellyn, the last of the Lakes' three thousand foot mountains. Helvellyn is the big attraction for walkers and climbers, whilst the motorboat-free lake is loved by sailors and paddlers. Even the steamers seem relaxed and unhurried as they ply back and forth between the two little towns. Ullswater is my favourite lake, close by my home in Shap, and the place I photograph most often. I hope it remains as unhurried for many years to come.

Ullswater from the prow of the *Lady of the Lake*

Ullswater and Norfolk Island in early morning mist

Norfolk Island and Ullswater at sunrise

The boat house at Pooley Bridge

Angle Tarn, Patterdale

Angle Tarn, high above Patterdale, is considered by many to be the finest mountain tarn in the district. It has an interesting shoreline with little bays and coves, a jutting peninsular, grassy knolls from which to view the landscape and of course, an island. Beyond, the landscape reveals High Street, the great whaleback fell that the Romans used as a highway across the district and below is Martindale, home to possibly the largest herd of wild red deer in England – perhaps 500 in the herd although you will struggle to even spot one!

Grisedale Valley in Patterdale

The Grisedale Valley is the normal start of the hike up to Helvellyn's famous Striding Edge. But it is also overlooked by St Sunday Crag and walkers who take the time to traverse the length of the valley will find themselves at Grisedale Tarn, looking down on Grasmere.

Sheffield Pike from Keldas

A short, steep walk above Glenridding gives access to a stunning viewpoint overlooking Ullswater and the surrounding fells at Keldas. A little further on, a small and often muddy tarn, Lantys Tarn dammed at one end, leads into the Grisedale valley.

Opposite
Aira Force

Aira Force, situated beside the Ullswater road at Gowbarrow Park, is the highest waterfall in the Lake District and probably the most famous. The main force falls 70 feet from below a stone footbridge but very little of the surrounding landscape is natural. This is a Victorian park with dramatic waterfalls, arboretum and rock scenery. Crafted and cultivated by the Howard family of Greystoke Castle, in the 1780s they landscaped the area around the force as a pleasure garden, planting over half a million native and ornamental trees and establishing a network of tracks, footpaths and bridges. In 1846 the Howards created an arboretum below Aira Force, planting over 200 specimen firs, pines, spruces and cedars from around the world, including a Sitka Spruce, which has reached 118 feet high.

Aira Beck

115

Haweswater and High Street

Haweswater and Whelter Crags

Haweswater Reservoir and Riggindale

Haweswater, the most easterly of all the Lakes, is a reservoir created in 1929 after Parliament passed an Act giving Manchester Corporation permission to build the reservoir to supply water for the urban cities of north-west England. It was a controversial decision because the village of Mardale was forcibly removed and the residents re-settled as the valley began to flood. Nowadays, the valley is unoccupied save for the Haweswater Hotel and when the water level recedes in drought years visitors can once again roam the ruined streets of the lost village of Mardale. The exceptional beauty of the landscape continues to attract walkers and climbers to make the journey up the deserted valley, climb the hills and look down on the still waters.

South Lakeland

The Southern reaches of Cumbria are not really Lakeland at all. The Lake District National Park boundary finishes north of Kendal and only in a very few places does it actually reach towards the coastal estuaries of the Kent or the river valley of the Lune. Even so, it's South Lakeland District Council that oversees this region and the description seems to fit. Most of this area was not even in Cumbria until the county boundary changes of 1974, when the old counties of Westmorland and Cumberland morphed into Cumbria and swallowed up Lancashire's northern portion of Morecambe Bay, a change that is resented in places, even to this day. Lancashire's loss was Cumbria's gain. Morecambe Bay is recognised as one of the most unique, wild habitats in Europe for a wide range of wading birds, wildfowl, flora and fauna, shellfish and molluscs – not to mention the landscape itself.

From Barrow-in-Furness east, the coast has been shaped by the relentless shifting and changing of the tidal channels, mud flats and sand banks that make up the outflows of the Crake and Leven, emptying from Coniston and Windermere, and the River Kent flowing from Kendal. The history of the bay is one of fishing, shipping, industry and tourism, each waxing and waning as the conditions changed – geographic, social and economic. Right now the emphasis is on tourism and conservation. The environmental importance of Morecambe Bay has been thrust into the spotlight with off shore wind farms and a new scheme to build a bridge across the bay. The idea isn't new – George Stevenson suggested it in 1834, but modern developments and a concern for the environmental impact have led to the idea of a "green" low-impact scheme that harnesses tidal action to generate power for the national grid. Such a bridge would inevitably change the character of South Lakeland forever, just as the coming of the railways did in the 1800s. Economically it could signal a boom time for Cumbria's relatively isolated southern shores. Time will tell – if it ever happens at all.

Although the seaside towns of Ulverston, Grange-over-Sands and Arnside were traditionally a part of Lancashire, Kendal and Kirkby Lonsdale were Westmorland towns with centuries of history written into the fabric of the buildings and streets. Sedbergh was formerly a part of the West Riding of Yorkshire. Now they are all part of Cumbria but they carry their identities, history and cultures as independently as ever. So South Lakeland has became something of a melting pot where history, industry, tourism and culture has been in constant flux since the Dark Ages and new developments look set to continue that change into the future.

Opposite
Bardsea, Holy Trinity church
The commanding church of Holy Trinity, stands overlooking Ulverston sands and Morecambe Bay on the edge of Bardsea village. It seems a very grand church, with important stained glass windows for such a small fishing community but Bardsea once played a vital role in the transport of iron ore to Fleetwood and Liverpool by steam ship. Now it has retreated back to a quiet seaside village, popular with coastal walkers and tourists.

Ulverston

The market town of Ulverston retains its traditional cobble sets throughout the market place and surrounding streets which have changed little over the last century. It would still look familiar to Ulverston's most famous son, Stan Laurel, who was born here in 1890. A Laurel and Hardy museum is run by enthusiasts in the town and draws visitors from around the world.

Victorian tea shops in Grange-over-Sands

A railway link across the Kent Estuary brought Victorian visitors in droves to Grange and the little town rapidly expanded. Grange-over-Sands still reflects its Victorian heyday when it was touted as the "Torquay of the North". Tourists arrived from Lancashire's industrial towns when Grange was still a part of Lancashire, to enjoy the sun and sand. Nowadays, the town is quieter and a little faded but there are still reminders of the old days and the town is proud of its heritage.

Grange-over-Sands promenade
The long, stately promenade – a full mile in length – is a slightly surreal presence along the "sea front" because the sea is nowhere to be seen! The Kent Estuary and Morecambe Bay is a vast, shifting inter-tidal zone that ebbs and flows over the years. The sea used to come right up to the foot of the prom but sadly does so no longer. Salt marsh and tough, salt loving grasses have taken over and muddy channels and drainage ditches meander through it all. That could all change again of course and the high tide might once again lap against the sea defence.

The Netherwood Hotel, Grange-over-Sands

The Netherwood was originally built as a family home for the Deakin family – rich industrialists who made a fortune in cotton, in the late 1800s. This was a building that was designed to make a statement. Absurdly grand and ostentatious, the 11 acre site was well chosen, with spectacular views out across Grange-over-Sands and Morecambe Bay.

Humphrey Head and Morecambe Bay

Humphrey Head lies just outside the remote fishing village of Flookburgh, named curiously enough after the local flatfish, "flukes" that are found out in the bay – or so they say. The limestone headland that juts out into the sands has been a protected site for many years now and is managed by Cumbria Wildlife Trust but is still a popular destination for walkers, bird watchers and even rock climbers. Venturing out onto the sands at low tide can be hazardous; the 18 cockle pickers who drowned in the bay in 2004 were not the first to be caught by the racing tide. Local cockle pickers have an intimate knowledge of the shifting sands and there has been a guide, by royal appointment, to lead parties from Grange to Arnside on the opposite shore since 1536. Cedric Robinson is the incumbent guide and has been since 1963.

Sandside and the Kent Estuary

The River Kent empties into Morecambe Bay at Arnside, creating a shifting pattern of creeks and channels that have widened and narrowed, silted and deepened as the centuries passed. The small village of Sandside, just upriver, once looked out over merchant ships grounded on the soft mud, with loading and unloading of cargo via barrows and carts at slack tide. Now of course, all that is gone, leaving behind a tranquil waterside village with a peaceful outlook toward the Lakeland hills.

The Kent Estuary at Arnside

Arnside itself is another Cumbrian town with a long history of shipping and trade, now vanished. Like all the South Lakeland ports fringing Morecambe Bay, Arnside was a Lancashire town until the boundary changes of 1974 but change had already affected the town long before that. The railway viaduct that spans the Kent Estuary brought tourism to the town in 1857 but it also led to the silting up of the shipping channel. Tourism replaced trade and Arnside still thrives as both seaside retreat and important wildlife refuge for wading and wetland birds.

A heron watches for fish at Arnside
With the evening lights of Kents Bank opposite, this heron waits and watches patiently for the splash of a fish on the shoreline of Arnside at low tide. The area around Arnside is an important habitat and breeding ground for many species of wading birds and wildfowl and is protected an Area of Outstanding Natural Beauty.

The end of a day's climbing at Farelton Knott

Farelton Knott and Hutton Roof are the first crags to be seen, perched above the M6 motorway as drivers cross the Lancashire/Cumbria border. Not many will take the time to explore these limestone pavements; local walkers know all about them, so do rock climbers. The uplifted edges form short, challenging problems for climbers with the attraction of a short walk-in and far reaching views across Morecambe Bay, which is surprisingly close by. Like many upland limestone areas, there are rare plants thriving up here too.

The Mushroom viewpoint, Scout Scar, Kendal

Scout Scar forms a sudden, sheer limestone barrier separating Kendal from the Lythe Valley. The unobstructed view towards Morecambe Bay to the south west and the Lakeland hills to the north west make it an ideal viewpoint and this oddly shaped stone viewing seat is known locally as the "Mushroom". A panoramic illustration, with place names, is etched into the inner lip of the roof.

Kendal from the A6 Shap road

Kendal was never the county town of Westmorland but it is certainly the most important. Historically, Kendal has been a stronghold since the Romans built a fort here and it has been said that it might easily have grown to become as important as York, indeed the parish church is only a few feet narrower than York Minster.

Kendal Castle

Catherine Parr, the sixth and final wife of Henry VIII, was the daughter of Sir Thomas Parr of Kendal Castle but was probably born in London and not Kendal as is so often quoted. A castle has existed on this site since the late twelfth century and at one stage Kendal had two castles. An early castle once stood at Castle Howe overlooking the town and the earthworks can still be seen. Kendal Castle itself has been landscaped and stabilised and is now a popular attraction.

Branthwaite Brow, Kendal market place
The defining characteristic of Kendal is its narrow yards and winding alleys, designed to be gated and guarded against attack. Branthwaite Brow itself is not a yard but leads to some interesting examples including one with seventeenth-century wood panelling and a curious shop front made of cast iron plates – designed to take up less room when the lane was widened in the mid 1800s. It's a miracle that so many of Kendal's historic yards have survived the destructive modernising zealots of the 1960s and '70s but fortunately they have.

The Mason's Arms, Strawberry Bank

Strawberry Bank is steep barrier that separates the southern end of Windermere from the Lythe Valley and sitting right on its tight hairpin corner is the Mason's Arms. This traditional, cosy, Lakeland pub has something of a reputation for both food and drink. It has its own micro-brewery and sells damson beer in the season, a local speciality of the Lythe Valley where damson growing is celebrated at the annual damson fair.

Damson tree in blossom, Lythe Valley

The Westmorland Damson is a member of the plum family and its name is said to derive from "Damascus" from where the trees originated. Nearly every farm and cottage in the Lythe Valley has a damson orchard, producing a riot of white blossom throughout the valley in springtime. Damson Day is held at Easter each year to celebrate and promote the diverse products that are derived from the fruit: damson wine, damson, gin, damson jam and chutney – the list is long. The reason why it's only here, in South Lakeland, is down to the limestone environment in which damson trees thrive.

Sedbergh town

Nestling at the foot of the Howgill Fells, Sedbergh has been a traditional dales market town since the 1200s – a long history indeed. The town is famous for its public school which was founded in 1525 but in recent years has re-invented itself as a "book town" with many antique book shops and an annual book fair. Sedbergh was not actually part of Cumbria at all until the reorganisation of county boundaries in 1974, but it still lies within the Yorkshire Dales National Park.

The Howgills after a winter storm

The Howgills are low, rolling fells that lie mostly within the Yorkshire Dales National Park. However, the southern Howgill Fells lie just within the Cumbrian border and are extremely popular with walkers, mountain bikers and fell runners. The western edge of the Howgills is bounded by the River Lune and the M6 motorway and it's these fells that make the M6 journey north towards Tebay such a spectacularly scenic route. Seen from Shap summit on the A6, the Howgills are often subject to sudden winter storms, the same weather that plagues the motorway itself.

Devils Bridge, Kirkby Lonsdale

The River Lune skirts the eastern edge of the Cumbrian/Yorkshire border and where it passes through the historic market town of Kirkby Lonsdale, a narrow gorge squeezes the river under this ancient, thirteenth-century bridge, now a scheduled monument. Devils Bridge is well known for other reasons too – during the summer months, this is one of the North's most popular motorcycle meeting points with hundreds of bikers converging here at weekends, making quite a spectacle. The name is mythical – many bridges have a similar tale attached – the devil built a bridge in exchange for the first soul across but a woman threw bread for her dog who chased after it, outwitting the devil.